Contents

Mary Cassatt 4

Timeline 6

Fun Facts 7

Young Mary 8

Going to Europe 10

Start of a Career 12

Trouble at Home 14

Off to France! 16

The Salon 18

Traveling Artist 20

Exploring Europe 22

Impressionists 24

Everyday People 26

Last Years 28

Glossary 30

Saying It 31

Web Sites 31

Index 32

Mary Cassatt

Mary Cassatt was a famous American artist. She was born in the United States. But for most of her life, Cassatt lived and worked in Paris, France.

Cassatt had many artist friends in Paris. These artists were called the Impressionists. They painted scenes of everyday life. They did not paint gods or goddesses, like other painters did. Instead, Impressionists painted real people doing ordinary things.

Like the other Impressionists, Cassatt also painted everyday scenes. She is most famous for her paintings of mothers and children. These works are warm and loving scenes from the daily lives of women.

When Cassatt was alive, there were not a lot of women artists. Many people thought that women could not paint as well as men. Cassatt showed the world that women could be good artists, too. Today, she is remembered as one of America's greatest artists.

A newspaper once described Mary Cassatt simply as "sister of Mr. Cassatt, President of the Pennsylvania Railroad," and owner of "the smallest Pekingese dog in the world." She would soon be known for more than just her relatives and dog!

Timeline

1844 ~ On May 22, Mary Cassatt was born in Allegheny City, Pennsylvania.

1860 ~ Cassatt began attending the Pennsylvania Academy of the Fine Arts in Philadelphia.

1865 ~ Cassatt and her mother traveled to France.

1868 ~ The Salon in Paris accepted *A Mandolin Player*.

1870 ~ Cassatt returned to the United States.

1871 ~ A Catholic bishop commissioned Cassatt to copy two paintings by Correggio in Parma, Italy.

1872 ~ Cassatt painted *During Carnival* and *The Bacchante*.

1877 ~ Cassatt's parents settled in Paris with her and Lydia.

1878 ~ Cassatt painted *Little Girl in a Blue Armchair*.

1893 ~ Cassatt painted a mural for the Women's Building at the World's Columbian Exposition.

1926 ~ On June 14, Cassatt died in Paris.

Fun Facts

 Mary Cassatt claimed that her father once said he would rather see her dead than see her become an artist! But, she always had her family's support as she grew in her career.

Cassatt first saw an Edgar Degas painting in a gallery window in Paris. She pressed her face to the glass so she could look at the painting very closely.

Cassatt once took two paintings to show in the Midwest. They were shown in a jewelry store and were destroyed in the Great Chicago Fire of 1871.

Before the end of her life, Cassatt burned all of her letters from Degas. So, some parts of their relationship remain a mystery.

The mural that Cassatt painted for the World's Columbian Exposition is now lost. The work challenged Cassatt, and she decided when it was finished that it was "beastly."

Young Mary

Mary Stevenson Cassatt was born on May 22, 1844, in Allegheny City, Pennsylvania. Today, Allegheny City is part of Pittsburgh, Pennsylvania.

Mary's parents had strong, outgoing personalities. Mary's father, Robert, had once been mayor of Allegheny City. He also worked as an investment banker. Mary's mother, Katherine, had a good education. This was unusual for women during the 1840s. She could speak and read French.

The family was very close. Mary had three brothers and one sister. Lydia, Alexander, and Robert were older than Mary. Her brother Gardner was

Cassatt's self-portrait shows her as a child.

younger. The children all enjoyed playing together and spending time with their parents.

Mary's parents could afford to give their children a good education and a comfortable life. They also wanted their children to experience life in other countries. They thought the children could get a better education in Europe, too. So, the Cassatts decided to move.

One of Cassatt's favorite subjects to paint was her family. This is Cassatt's portrait of her father.

Going to Europe

In 1851, Mary was seven years old. That year, the Cassatt family moved to Paris. The family lived in an elegant apartment. They all learned a lot in France, including how to speak French. Mary was especially good at learning new languages.

Mary loved living in Paris. She enjoyed visiting the city's parks. She also loved going to the museums around the city. Paris had many beautiful art collections. Mary spent hours looking at the art of Paris.

In 1853, the Cassatts moved to Germany. Two years later, Mary's brother Robbie died of a joint disease. He was 13 years old. The family was very sad and did not want to live in Europe anymore. By the end of 1855, they were back in Pennsylvania.

Cassatt's painting of her brother Robbie and their father

This painting by David Carey pictures one of the most famous art museums in Paris, the Louvre.

Start of a Career

Mary went to school when her family returned from Europe. But, her family concentrated more on her brothers' education than on Mary's. Still, she became committed to studying art.

When Mary was 16, she began taking classes at the Pennsylvania **Academy** of the Fine Arts in Philadelphia. Mary learned many important things at the academy. She learned about proportion, colors, and **technique**. She studied human **anatomy** and copied **casts** of the human body.

Mary quickly grew tired of all the rules she had to follow for her teachers. She wanted to express herself by painting in her own style. Some said that only men could be painters. They thought that women should create art only as a hobby. But Mary wanted a career as a painter.

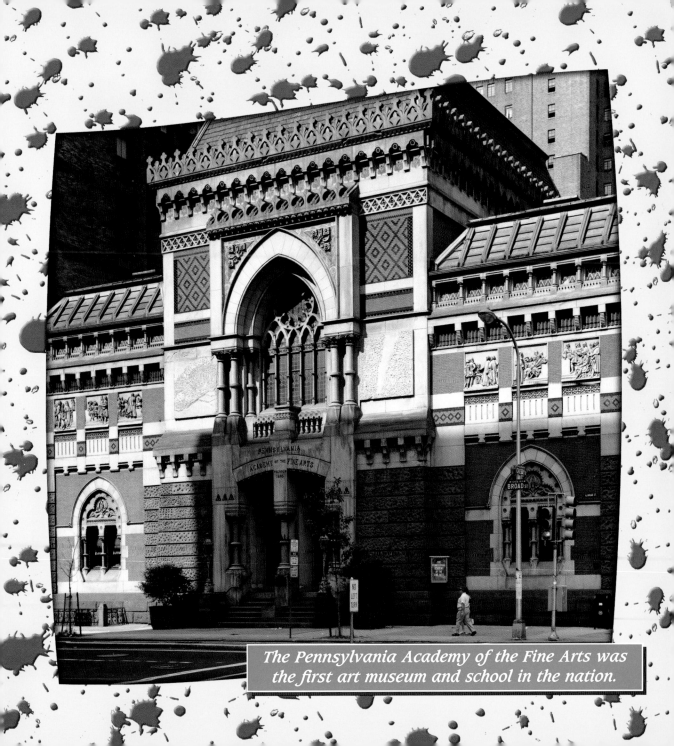

The Pennsylvania Academy of the Fine Arts was the first art museum and school in the nation.

Trouble at Home

In the late 1800s, women were expected to marry and have children. They were supposed to run the household. It was unusual for a woman to have a career outside the home.

Mary thought it would be easier to paint for a living in Europe. She knew art was everywhere there. It was easy to see famous paintings in museums. Artwork was even displayed on the streets. Mary did not feel that she could learn to be a great artist if she didn't live in Europe.

It was very unusual for a family to send a girl abroad by herself. Also, in the early 1860s, the United States was divided by the **Civil War**. So, the U.S. government had put limits on travel. There were many obstacles between Mary and Europe.

Paris in the 1800s was a gathering place for painters who often sold their art on the street.

Cassatt painted her mother reading the French newspaper Le Figaro. Although women were expected to take care of the home, Cassatt's mother was also educated and served as a role model for her.

Off to France!

When the **Civil War** was over, Mary was finally able to return to Europe. She and her mother sailed to France in late 1865. Mary's best friend, Eliza Haldeman, also went to France. Haldeman wanted to be a painter, too. When Mary's mother went home, Mary and Eliza were on their own.

Mary spent many hours looking at the paintings in the Paris museums. The best museum was the Louvre. It displayed some of the most famous paintings in the world.

One of the best art schools in Paris was the École des Beaux-Arts. However, women were not allowed to study there. So, Mary began

Edgar Degas painted Mary Cassatt (right) visiting the Louvre.

taking lessons from Jean-Léon Gérome. Gérome was a very respected painter. It was a great honor to be his student.

In 1867, Mary and Eliza moved to the French countryside. From there, the women could still visit museums in the city. However, in the country they were able to paint the villagers. Mary especially enjoyed painting French peasants.

In the mid-1800s, Cassatt was a fashionable young woman. She had a carte-de-visite with this photo on it. These cards were often exchanged on birthdays and holidays.

The Salon

One of the best places for artists to exhibit their paintings was at the Paris Salon. The Salon held a contest every year. Painters from all over France sent their work to the Salon judges.

The Salon judges rejected many paintings. It was a great honor to have a painting chosen for the Salon. The annual exhibit provided artists with a large audience. Many artists sold their work to people who had attended.

At first, Cassatt's paintings were rejected by the Salon. Finally, in 1868, a painting of a girl playing a **mandolin** was accepted. It was called *A Mandolin Player.* At last, Cassatt's work would be exhibited at the Salon. Cassatt later had several more paintings accepted by the judges.

At this time, France was at war with Prussia, which is now part of Germany. So, Paris was not a safe place. Despite her recent success, Cassatt decided to go home to Pennsylvania.

Much of Paris was burned during the Franco-Prussian War. But, the city that emerged afterward would again be an attraction to artists.

Traveling Artist

Cassatt did not want to leave Paris. However, she knew she would be safer in Philadelphia. In 1870, she arrived home and set up a studio near her family's house. She began painting pictures of her family. Cassatt's mother and her sister Lydia were her favorite **subjects**.

But, the Cassatt family soon moved to a **suburb** outside of Philadelphia. Cassatt grew lonely there. And, she found it harder to get art supplies.

Finally in 1871, Cassatt received a request to travel to Parma, Italy. A Catholic bishop in Pittsburgh wanted her to copy two paintings by an Italian painter known as Correggio.

The bishop wanted these copies to hang in Pittsburgh's St. Paul Cathedral. Cassatt was very excited and said yes to the bishop. Now she could go back to Europe!

Many of Cassatt's family paintings are of her sister, Lydia, including The Reader (top) and a profile of Lydia (bottom).

Exploring Europe

Cassatt enjoyed copying Correggio's work. She studied the way Correggio used light and shadow to make his figures look dramatic. However, she only finished painting *Coronation of the Virgin*.

Now that she was back, Cassatt traveled all over Europe. She studied paintings in museums and cathedrals. In Spain, Cassatt studied great painters such as Diego Velázquez. In 1872, Cassatt painted two works that were very well liked in Europe. They were called *During Carnival* and *The Bacchante*.

Cassatt also enjoyed spending time in Holland. She learned a great deal by studying different artists in these countries. In 1874, she permanently settled in Paris, where her sister, Lydia, joined her.

Over the next few years, Cassatt became well known in France. She sold many works of art. However, she was also **criticized** for using bright colors and for painting modern women. But, Cassatt did not get discouraged. She wanted to do something new.

The dark colors used by many Spanish painters can be seen in Cassatt's The Bacchante.

Impressionists

In the late 1870s, Cassatt met a French painter named Edgar Degas. Degas painted with light-colored pastels. Cassatt admired his work very much. Degas also liked the way Cassatt painted. The two became very good friends.

After seeing her work, Degas suggested that Cassatt join a group of painters called the Impressionists. The Impressionists did not paint many historical scenes or pictures of gods and goddesses. They painted what they saw every day. This was exactly Cassatt's style.

Many people did not like Impressionist paintings. They thought the style was sloppy and too colorful. But Cassatt enjoyed working with the Impressionists. She stopped sending her work to the Salon. The Impressionists held their own shows. For these, Cassatt could paint what she wanted.

In 1877, Cassatt's parents settled in Paris with her and Lydia. Cassatt could again use her family as **subjects**. And, she had other people to help with chores while she concentrated on her art.

By 1881, Cassatt had an art dealer named Paul Durand-Ruel. He helped sell her paintings. Cassatt also found friends in Europe and America to buy Impressionist paintings.

At first, the Impressionists called themselves the Independents. A journalist came up with the Impressionist name. He got the idea from a painting by Claude Monet called Impression: Sunrise.

Everyday People

After joining the Impressionists, Cassatt was free to develop her own style. Part of this style was the natural look of her **subjects**. This can be seen in *Little Girl in a Blue Armchair,* which she had painted in 1878. But, not everyone liked the painting at that time. In fact, it was rejected at an exhibition.

Cassatt enjoyed painting her subjects in ordinary situations. Some of her pictures showed women fixing their hair or sewing. In these pictures, the subjects are not looking at the painter. They don't even seem to know they are being painted.

Cassatt became famous for her paintings of mothers and children. Some paintings show a mother giving her child a bath. Others show a woman holding or touching a child. These works are full of love and warmth.

It is obvious from Cassatt's paintings that she loved children. However, she never had any of her own. Instead, she showed her love for children by creating beautiful paintings of them.

Artist's Corner

Many aspects of Impressionist painting can be seen in Cassatt's *Little Girl in a Blue Armchair*.

For example, the Impressionists liked to paint unposed scenes from everyday life. In this painting, the little girl is not sitting up straight. She is slouched in the chair with her skirt pulled up. Cassatt painted her the way a child really would sit.

The colors and texture of the painting also show the Impressionist influence. Heavy brushstrokes add texture to the painting. The colors are not the reds and greens used to portray the gods of classical paintings. They are bright and exciting.

Last Years

Later in her career, Cassatt tried different styles of painting. In 1893, she painted a huge **mural** of women for the Women's Building at the World's Columbian Exposition. Cassatt was finally one of the most respected painters in Europe. In later years, she enjoyed growing popularity in America, as well.

In her later years, Cassatt experimented with new techniques and influences. One of Cassatt's new interests was printmaking, or reproducing paintings. She was moved by Japanese prints especially. A Japanese touch can be seen in many of Cassatt's paintings, such as The Letter. *Here, the background is very important, as it is in Japanese prints. Still, the painting is two-dimensional and flat looking. Most importantly,* The Letter *and the Japanese prints that influenced Cassatt presented women in a careful, respectful way.*

In the late 1800s and early 1900s, Cassatt was heartbroken by the loss of many family members. Her father died in 1891. Her mother and sister also died by 1895. By 1911, both of her brothers had died.

Cassatt also worried about her own health. In 1915, she began losing her eyesight. Cassatt died in her adopted home of Paris on June 14, 1926. She was 82 years old.

Mary Cassatt's popularity continued after her death. Her paintings made everyday activities seem special and important. Bright colors and heavy brushstrokes made her paintings lively and exciting. Today, she holds an important place in the history of art.

Cassatt's failing eyesight made it harder for her to paint in her later years.

Glossary

academy - a private school that trains students in a specific field.

anatomy - the branch of science that deals with the structure of the body.

cast - a shape formed when material is molded to and then separated from an object.

civil war - a war between groups in the same country. The United States of America and the Confederate States of America fought a civil war from 1861 to 1865.

criticize - to find fault with something.

mandolin - a stringed musical instrument.

mural - a picture painted on a wall or ceiling.

subject - the focus of a work of art, such as a person.

suburb - the towns or villages just outside a city.

technique - a method or style in which something is done.

Saying It

Allegheny - a-luh-GAY-nee
Bacchante - buh-KANT
Cassatt - kuh-SAT
Correggio - kohr-RAYD-joh
Diego Velázquez - DYAY-goh bay-LAHTH-kayth
École des Beaux-Arts - ay-KOLE DAY bohz-AHR
Edgar Degas - ED-gahr duh-GAH
Jean-Léon Gérome - ZHAHN-LAY-OHN ZHAY-ROHM
Louvre - LOOV
Parma - PAHR-mah

Web Sites

To learn more about Mary Cassatt, visit ABDO Publishing Company on the World Wide Web at **www.abdopub.com**. Web sites about Cassatt are featured on our Book Links page. These links are routinely monitored and updated to provide the most current information available.

Index

A

Allegheny City, Pennsylvania 8

B

Bacchante, The 22

C

Civil War, U.S. 14, 16

Coronation of the Virgin 22

Correggio 20, 22

D

Degas, Edgar 24

Durand-Ruel, Paul 25

During Carnival 22

E

École des Beaux-Arts 16

F

family 8, 9, 10, 12, 16, 20, 22, 25, 29

France 10, 16, 17, 18, 22, 24

G

Germany 10, 18

Gérome, Jean-Léon 17

H

Haldeman, Eliza 16, 17

Holland 22

I

Impressionism 4, 24, 25, 26

L

Little Girl in a Blue Armchair 26

Louvre 16

M

Mandolin Player, A 18

P

Paris, France 4, 10, 16, 20, 22, 25, 29

Paris Salon 18, 24

Parma, Italy 20

Pennsylvania 10, 18

Pennsylvania Academy of the Fine Arts 12

Philadelphia, Pennsylvania 12, 20

Pittsburgh, Pennsylvania 8, 20

Prussia 18

S

Spain 22

St. Paul Cathedral 20

V

Velázquez, Diego 22

W

World's Columbian Exposition 28